Discover Your Corporate Strengths & Beat the Competition

Book One of the Seven Book Series on: Secrets to Unlock Profit and Inspire Employees

By

Richard A Melancon, CPA

First Edition

Copyright © 2018 by Richard A Melancon, CPA
All rights reserved.

Reproduction or translation of any part of this work beyond that permitted by Section 107 or 108 of the 1976 United States Copyright Act without the permission of the copyright owner is unlawful. Please address all requests for permission or further information to:

> Permissions Department
> Melancon Consulting
> P O Box 8426
> Metairie, LA 70011-8426

This publication is designed to provide accurate and authoritative information about the subject matter covered. It is sold with the understanding that the publisher is not engaged in rendering legal, accounting, or other professional services. If legal advice or other expert assistance is required, please seek the services of a competent professional.

INTRODUCTION 5

CHAPTER 1 SWOT ANALYSIS 7

SWOT CONCEPTS ---2
INTERNAL VS. EXTERNAL FACTORS---5
STRENGTHS---7
WEAKNESSES---8
OPPORTUNITIES---9
THREATS---10
BENEFITS OF SWOT ANALYSIS---11
ABILITY TO SET REALISTIC GOALS---12
PROACTIVE PLANNING---13
BUDGETING WITH A PURPOSE---15
MANAGED GROWTH---15
SUSTAINABLE OPERATIONS---16
ABILITY TO OPEN OUTLETS EFFICIENTLY---16
BUSINESS PLAN---18
STRATEGIC PLAN---27
BUDGETING PROCESS---28
CAPITAL BUDGET---34
PROJECT BUDGET---36
CONCLUSION---41

CHAPTER 2 FINDING THE MONEY 43

PERSONAL SAVINGS---43
FAMILY LOAN---45
BANK LOANS---48
CREDIT CARDS---52
INVESTOR CAPITAL---53
FINANCING DECISIONS IMPACT EMPLOYEES-54
CONCLUSION---56

INTRODUCTION

As entrepreneurs, we want to believe that our business will sustain us for many years. In fact, this belief is necessary to accept the daily challenges that every business owner must face. Will someone steal my customers? Will I have enough cash to make payroll this week? Will I have any profit to pay my personal mortgage this month? These are common concerns for all owners of start-up companies.

In this book, we explore ways for you to define the core strengths of your business and to look objectively at your key challenges. Through this examination, you can build your business based on your unique assets and steer away from those encounters that could cause you to lose profit.

The second major topic area in this book is to identify the sources of funding available to the company. Everyone knows that banks lend money. But, most new owners are surprised by the many rules and roadblocks that banks create to inhibit the loan approval process.

In closing, thank you for purchasing this book. It is always a good idea to learn as much as you can about the areas that interest you the most. Since you are in business or about to be in business, this should be your key area of focus until your business is sustainable.

As you read each section of this book, consider how you will implement the key concepts in your business. If fact, you should consider making handwritten notes while you read this book. Underline the sentences that are meaningful to you. Write in the margin. Write your plans on a separate sheet of paper. Whatever works for you to follow through on your ideas that are inspired by the passages in this book.

Chapter 1
SWOT Analysis

When you're ready to take an objective look at your business, consider the SWOT Analysis as your starting point. SWOT is an acronym that stands for: a) Strengths, b) Weaknesses, c) Opportunities, and d) Threats. Use the SWOT analysis to assess the status of your business regarding these four areas of your business.

There are many books on SWOT analysis, and there are consultants that focus their entire effort on helping clients perform this analysis. These resources are available because a SWOT analysis can be a very important task for you and your company to complete each year. However, you probably should not delegate this analysis to others within your company without your direct involvement at some level.

The SWOT analysis is used to determine:
- What are the most positive attributes of your company (strengths),
- In what areas do you need to improve the most (weaknesses),
- Where do you believe are your next source(s) of new revenue (opportunities), and
- How will the competition or environmental factors adversely affect your ability to succeed (threats).

A recent search on Google® reviewed the following tools that you can use to perform a SWOT analysis for your company.

Discover Your Corporate Strengths & Beat The Competition

www.mindjet.com Mindjet SWOT Template for MindManager software

www.strat-pro.com SWOT PowerPoint templates to present SWOT concepts within your company

www.businessballs.com SWOT Analysis template in Microsoft® Word®

www.mindtools.com SWOT Analysis Worksheet for use with the MindTools products

www.valuebasedmanagement.net/methodsswotanalysis.html Explanation of the SWOT analysis and a template to perform the assessment.

Discover Your Company's Strengths & Beat The Competition

SWOT CONCEPTS

SWOT is a structured approach to help you assess the positive outcome of a specific project or to review the competitive position of your company. SWOT analysis allows you to seek input from your staff, customers, or external consultants, using easily understood directions. For example, if you were to survey recent customers to determine their view of your strengths, you could ask the following questions to recent buyer:

1. Please rate the two most significant reasons why you purchased the product(s) from our store today:
   _____ Price
   _____ Availability of inventory
   _____ Location of Store
   _____ Reputation of company
   _____ Verified Product Quality
   _____ Recent advertising
   _____ Discount Coupon

Discover Your Company's Strengths & Beat The Competition

2. Please tell us how the main reason for choosing the product(s) from our company:
   _____ Innovative Design
   _____ Color Selection
   _____ Availability of Stock
   _____ Discounted Price
   _____ Value
   _____ Market Leader
   _____ Easy-carry packaging

3. Please select from the list below the improvement(s) that you would like to see in our next version of the product:
   _____ More features
   _____ More sizes
   _____ Greater Availability (Purchased online because local stores do not carry your item)
   _____ Family-size package
   _____ Less Weight. Slimmer Design

4. Please describe why you purchased the item(s) from our company:
   _____
   _____

Using the survey approach, you can identify patterns of consistency to determine your strengths and then use that information to set goals to maintain or improve upon these strengths.

Similarly, you can survey your staff to ask questions that can lead to new and creative solutions to current problems. Whenever possible, employees should be encouraged to provide meaningful feedback to the owner so that everyone is part of the success of the business.

Discover Your Corporate Strengths & Beat The Competition

Samples questions for employees to address may include:

1. What is your highest priority in your job? Specifically, what are the activities that you perform that are necessary for the company to continue operating?

   _____
   _____
   _____

2. What are the biggest obstacles that keep you from completing your work?

   _____Work Compression (work load is not evenly spread throughout the week)
   _____Inadequate tools (Equipment no longer supports the volume of work)
   _____Lack of consistent procedures (Each employee completes projects differently)
   _____Frequent exceptions are approved by Supervisors (Employees know what to do, but they are allowed to ignore procedures upon request.)
   _____Other:
   _____

3. If you could change your work processes, what changes would you like to implement, and how would this affect other departments that provide information to you?

   _____
   _____
   _____

Discover Your Company's Strengths & Beat The Competition

The main benefit of the SWOT Analysis is to support the owner's proactive steps in managing the long-term success of the company. Successful owners recognize that market factors can reduce or eliminate profits in any single year. However, successful owners will address this issue by maintaining an adequate line of credit or cash reserves to cover expenses during these temporary down turns.

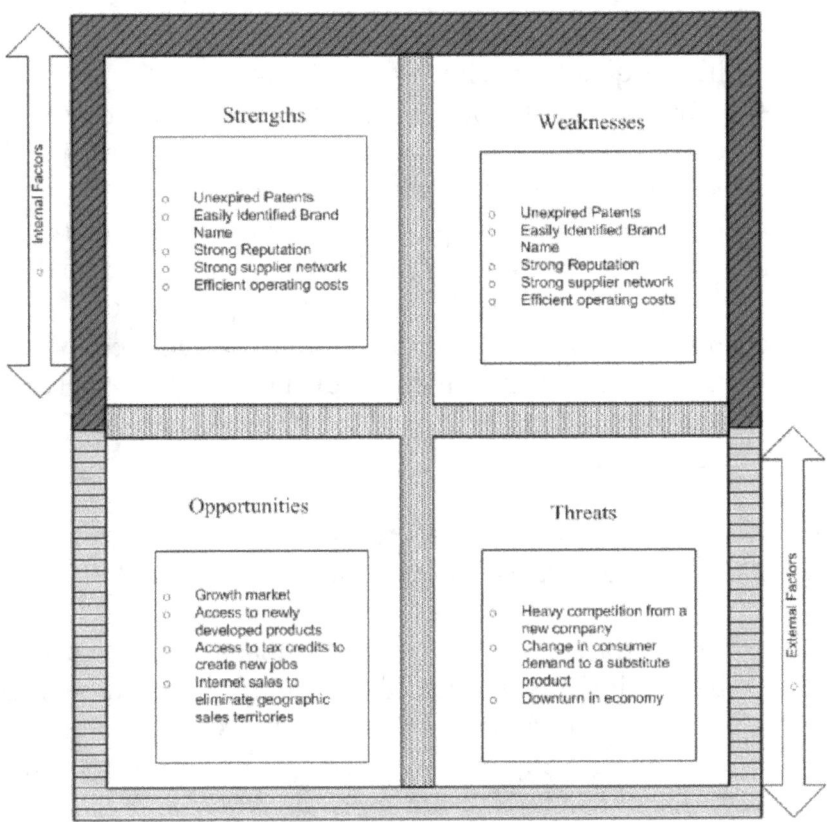

SWOT Analysis

INTERNAL VS. EXTERNAL FACTORS
One helpful method to analyze your SWOT findings is to segment the components into internal factors and external

Discover Your Corporate Strengths & Beat The Competition

factors. **Strengths** and **Weaknesses** are internal factors that tend to relate to attributes that are directly within your control over a short timeframe (1 – 5 years). Conversely, external issues are **Opportunities** and **Threats** that may be outside of your direct control.

At a more in-depth level, *internal factors* relate to areas of production, procedures, and daily operations. Examples of internal factors may include:

- Investing in production equipment (i.e., upgrading to higher quality machinery);
- Training staff and assessing performance (e.g., ensuring that employees follow procedures and interact appropriately with customers);
- Implementing appropriate marketing campaigns (e.g., ensuring that advertising is correctly placed in the media outlets and with sufficient frequency); or
- Installing store fixtures (store cleanliness and neatness, product merchandising on the shelves, uncluttered aisles, free flow of customer checkout lanes).

External factors reflect market conditions or regulatory restrictions. Examples of external factors may include:

- <u>Regulatory restrictions</u> that impact your industry (collecting the "Healthcare" tanning salon tax, paying for costs to comply with American with Disabilities Act rules, complying with air quality standards after renovating a manufacturing facility, etc.);
- <u>Competitive pressures</u> that cause you to reduce your prices and decrease your profit;
- <u>Technological advances</u> that cause your products to become obsolete.

Discover Your Company's Strengths & Beat The Competition

- ♦ <u>Decrease in customer base</u> due to an economic downturn in the area or a migration of residents after a significant event. (Such an outward migration occurred at a local level when over 200,000 Hurricane Katrina victims moved from New Orleans to other towns; in 2005; also, a larger migration occurred in California and Nevada after the collapse of that regional economy in 2008).

STRENGTHS
The strengths of your business include those factors that encourage customers to continue to buy your products or services. Typically, your strengths incorporate positive factors that help to make the buying experience a positive event for your customers. When customers are happy buying your products, they tend to buy from you again. Consider from your own perspective the number of times that you purchase items from a convenience store as opposed to buying from a full-service grocery store. Which one do you prefer to visit? Which store offers a faster buying experience? In which store is it easier to find your desired products?

For some companies, the major strength is the company's ability to relieve the customer's fear or install a sense of security. For example, customers hire a tax accountant to relieve the fear of filing a tax return with errors. People hire lawyers when they are sued because they do not want to lose their assets or their liberties. Homeowners often install a home security system to reduce the risk of a home intrusion.

When your customers purchase your services as a defensive tactic, you may want to look at factors beyond the quality of work to establish your competitive advantage. However, without feedback from your customers, you may overlook

Discover Your Corporate Strengths & Beat The Competition

the true strength of your products from the customer's perspective.

WEAKNESSES

Your corporate weaknesses tend to reflect your inability to change in response to the market's demands. For example, companies that do not upgrade their equipment, fixtures, hours of operation, or product line will see a diminishing sales level each year when competing companies offer longer operating hours, newer showrooms, or extended delivery schedules.

- Retailers that do not offer an internet buying option lose sales to competitors with an Internet store.
- Tax preparers who do not offer E-Filing options lose clients to preparers with more current systems.
- Retail circulars that are not addressed in the name of the current resident are quickly discarded as "Junk Mail" and provide no benefit to the company or the customer.

> ***Profit Opportunity***
> SWOT is a structured approach to help you assess the positive outcome of a specific project or to review the competitive position of your company.

Weaknesses can be ignored for a short period of time without adversely affecting sales. However, if you place a low priority on correcting the weaknesses within your organization, then you extend the time over which your company will operate with inferior practices and lower profit levels.

Discover Your Company's Strengths & Beat The Competition

OPPORTUNITIES

Opportunities are potential events or conditions that can create new revenue sources for existing products or allow you to offer new products to existing customers.

For example, when personal computers were first introduced into the consumer market, buyers were introduced to the dot matrix printer to create computer-generated letters. When digital cameras were developed, consumers quickly purchased an inkjet printer that could print letters and photographs. Consumers did not discard their dot matrix printers. Instead, they added a second inkjet printer to the existing computer, and thereby increased revenue for printer companies without impacting the sale of existing products (home computers).

> ***Profit Opportunity***
> If you place a low priority on correcting the weaknesses within your organization, then you extend the time over which your company will operate with inferior practices and lower profit levels.

An example of an opportunity for new revenue came to A T & T® when the Apple Computer Company® agreed to sell the Apple I-Phone® exclusively through the A T & T® cellular phone distribution network. Most of the buyers of the Apple I-Phone purchased a replacement phone, as opposed to a first-time cellular device.

As a result, A T & T® was able to earn revenue twice from these trend-setters. They initially purchased a cellular phone

Discover Your Corporate Strengths & Beat The Competition

(prior to the I-Phone rollout) and then purchased a smart phone – even though the cellular phone was fully operational.

It's important for you to recognize opportunities throughout the life of your company. It's equally important for you to separate positive opportunities from bad or false opportunities.

Beneficial opportunities can bring you new revenues, help you to reduce costs, or allow you to move your business in a new direction. False opportunities tend to be presented as deals, contracts, or products that you buy and the items fail to perform as represented.

THREATS

The threats to your business (within the context of the SWOT Analysis) refer to those factors that can cause your business to lose income, increase costs, reduce your customer base or restrict your ability to achieve your mission and goals.

> ***Profit Opportunity***
> Whenever possible, employees should be encouraged to provide meaningful feedback to the owner so that everyone is part of the success of the business.

Some of the threats that are common to many businesses at some point in their development include:

- Reduced customer base;
- Rising supplier costs;
- Higher fuel and transportation costs;
- New competitors in the market; and

Discover Your Company's Strengths & Beat The Competition

- Natural disasters that cause an interruption in production or delivery of goods.

BENEFITS OF SWOT ANALYSIS

Now that you understand the concepts behind the SWOT analysis, and the fact that you should update your analysis at least once each year, consider the following benefits that a company can achieve with a successful review:

- Ability to Set Realistic Goals Each Year

- Proactive planning whereby staff understand their role in the success of the company

- Budgeting with a purpose. Budgets can measure your success over time and can guide you in matching your operational output to market demands cost effectively.

- Managed growth. You should avoid revenue declines as well as hyper-growth. Ideally, the growth of your company should result in an incremental increase in revenue along with incremental changes in the structure of your operations.

- Sustainable operations. A company should avoid erratic sales patterns or cost spikes. A sustainable company is a valuable asset beyond its ability to earn revenue each month.

- Ability to open new outlets efficiently. Often, a company will grow by opening additional locations to serve new geographical markets. The SWOT analysis can help decide which of the target markets will yield a higher return on investment.

Discover Your Corporate Strengths & Beat The Competition

ABILITY TO SET REALISTIC GOALS

As stated above, SWOT Analysis divides the four components into internal vs. external factors. The internal factors (Strengths and Weaknesses) highlight the areas that are within your control to improve or modify within the short term (1 – 5 years). External factors (Opportunities and Threats) relate to areas controlled by the marketplace or by external forces, such as government regulators or technological advances.

Your company will have limited ability to adjust the external factors within the short term. However, you can adjust all aspects of your business over the long term. Therefore, if you are aware of pending opportunities or threats, you can implement strategic plans within the current cycle that allow you to profit from opportunities or avoid impending threats in future periods.

> ***Profit Opportunity***
> The strengths of your business include those factors that encourage customers to become motivated to continue buying your products or services. Typically, your strengths incorporate positive factors that help to make the buying experience a positive event for your customers.

For example, if you believe that one product in your catalog will become obsolete, you can begin negotiating with suppliers to begin selling an alternative product line at a future point. Such a transition will not be easy and will take more than a few months to implement fully, so this is probably a long-term project. Setting a strategy today will allow you to transition to the new product line faster so that you can sell the new products without delay.

Similarly, if you know of pending regulations that will restrict your ability to transport your products using a specific route or an identifiable carrier system (e.g., you may be barred from sending highly flammable products via air carrier), then you can search for alternatives now so that you will be ready to change your procedures if the legislation is enacted.

PROACTIVE PLANNING
One of the responsibilities of the owner or top management is to always take control during a crisis and to always be able to solve a business issue when a problem occurs. This is an absolute statement and one that every employee counts on when they arrive at work each day. It is also a goal that you will fail to achieve at some point in your career as an owner or an executive.

This conflicting reality is one of the causes of stress for the owner of any business. Typically, an entrepreneur will:

1) Start a business;
2) Operate with a clear direction;
3) Hire employees with specific duties;
4) Begin to sell the products or services to customers;
5) While maintaining an expectation of profits each month.

However, once the doors to the store are open, future planning often is suspended so that everyone can focus on "making the sale" and "creating success."

Keep in mind that the owner is responsible to update the strategic plan so that the long-term business growth will occur as anticipated. The frequency of changes to the strategic plan will depend on events and opportunities within the environment, but the plan must be reviewed and updated at least once each year to maintain its effectiveness.

This duty, along with other actions such as reviewing control reports (accounting statements, inventory reports, collection statistics, etc.), are examples of proactive planning within the business. The SWOT Analysis is another type of proactive planning because such an analysis requires you to look outside of the standard corporate reports and compile information that is beyond the assigned duties of most employees.

Since the SWOT Analysis is outside of the skill set for most employees, a company typically will perform a SWOT Analysis in conjunction with an outside consultant or facilitator. Keep in mind, however, that your employees should participate in the process for the following reasons.

- ♦ Employees know the current marketplace as well as, or better than, an outside consultant, and employees can provide a current assessment of changes in market demand.
- ♦ When you include staff in corporate planning, employees will gain comfort that you are in charge and that you are aware of the changes required to keep the company viable.
- ♦ Employees who contribute to the analysis will experience job enrichment and may feel empowered. They will know that they are part of the success of the business because you added their input into the final strategic plan.
- ♦ Including employees in your strategic planning sessions allows you to train, assess, and select the next leaders of your company based on their

performance, insight, contributions, and willingness to meet corporate goals.

BUDGETING WITH A PURPOSE
Detailed budgeting concepts are presented later in this section. In anticipation of presenting this concept, keep in mind that a budget is a tool to help you acquire the financial resources you need to implement changes that keep your business profitable. If you want to undertake new opportunities in the marketplace, then you'll need to implement strategic changes to your business. This enhancement will require a financial investment that may be beyond the level generated by monthly operations (e.g., building a new warehouse, replacing manufacturing equipment, opening a new office in a remote city, etc.).

The company budget can allow you to communicate to bankers or investors the value of potential opportunities and to show your ability to pay for the investment in advance of any new construction.

MANAGED GROWTH
The SWOT Analysis allows you to focus on and reinforce your strengths to ensure that your investment pays the greatest return in any market. If you allow your weaknesses to continue to absorb your resources or if you permit threats to become a menace to your business, you will lose profit and impede growth.

SUSTAINABLE OPERATIONS
Some owners will define their company goals with respect to the owner's personal goals. For example, if an owner is

Discover Your Corporate Strengths & Beat The Competition

beginning his/her career and family, then the business goals may be growth oriented. As the owner nears retirement age, the goals of the company may be oriented toward stability so that the owner can sell the company at maximum value to investors, competitors or employees.

In a down economy, most owners focus on goals to ensure that the company will survive past the economic downturn and then transition to a growth strategy during the economic recovery period.

The SWOT Analysis can assist in defining the goals that match the environment or the owner's needs over time. When the company fails to engage in sustainable business practices, then the company will fail over the near term (one to five years).

ABILITY TO OPEN OUTLETS EFFICIENTLY

One of the strategies for growth is to duplicate a successful company in a second location. The most common example is the model that franchise operators follow.

The owners of a company spend a great deal of effort defining and refining organizational policies, marketing strategies, operational procedures, hiring practices, etc. Once the owners are comfortable that they have developed a workable "model" for their business, they will find buyers who want to purchase the right to operate a new outlet of the company in a remote location. (Franchise agreements vary in the degree of the founder's influence and ownership in the new outlets.)

The main benefit of a SWOP Analysis is to define the four strategic areas of the business and then to assess whether these attributes will match the needs and the environment of

Discover Your Company's Strengths & Beat The Competition

a proposed market or location. For example, cellular phones were first introduced in the late 1980's as a consumer product. Retail stores were located in dense urban cities where more potential customers were easily identified, as opposed to rural locations.

In the early years of cellular telephone implementation, cell towers that were required to carry the telephone signal were expensive to build. Also, each network used a proprietary signal that could not be carried by a competing network so each carrier owned their unique towers. Finally, companies required high revenue volume to justify their high investment in the market so that they could earn a return on their capital outlay. For these reasons, cellular telephone companies were not encouraged to offer their services in locations with small populations, mountainous terrain, or significant competition.

Technology has changed since the early years of cellular service and to allow all cellular companies to use any tower. This has opened new opportunities for a few companies to focus on building tower sites that they can rent to all cellular companies. This new opportunities allows cellular companies to focus their capital on improving their cell phones and data services without the need to invest in cell towers. The tower companies can invest in cell towers in rural areas that can be used by any carrier to serve new customers who were unserved when each company has to use a proprietary cell tower signal.

The SWOT Analysis can help you determine whether a potential opportunity is valid for your organization in a remote location. As an example, when MacDonald's Corporation builds a new restaurant you will quickly see other fast food restaurants appear within walking distance of the original MacDonald's Restaurant. This is because MacDonald's corporation takes great effort in finding a town

Discover Your Corporate Strengths & Beat The Competition

that will support its operations profitably in light of eventual competition.

Conversely, when you see a Church's Fried Chicken restaurant in a neighborhood, you will probably not see a Popeye's Fried Chicken restaurant in the same general area. This is because the internal SWOT Analysis shows that the Church's franchise tends to attract a different market segment than the Popeye's franchise, even though both restaurants offer similar products on their menu.

BUSINESS PLAN

Once you have updated your SWOT analysis, the next step is to update your business plan to reflect the actions that you will take to apply your strengths, explore your opportunities, diminish your weaknesses, or minimize the threats. According to Wikipedia, a business plan is: a) a formal statement of a set of business goals, b) the reasons why the targets are attainable, and c) the anticipated approach to reach those objectives. It may also contain background information about the organization or team that is attempting to reach the goals.

The Wikipedia definition is a reasonable working definition of a business plan, but this limited description does not indicate the elements that must be present in the business plan for it to have significant value to the organization.

A Business Plan should be your description of: a) what your business will look like, b) how it will function (daily operations), c) the types of products and services it will offer, and d) the description of the customers it will serve. The business plan should create a descriptive picture of your business over each of the next five years. For example, if you anticipate opening one store or office in the first year and then expand to two additional centers in the fourth year, then that information should be in your business plan. The elements of a comprehensive business plan include:

- ✓ Executive Summary
- ✓ Mission Statement
- ✓ Market Analysis
- ✓ Company Description
- ✓ Organization and Staffing
- ✓ Marketing Plan
- ✓ Service or products (to help identify positive opportunities or to reduce the risk of implementing false opportunities)
- ✓ Initial Capital Budget
- ✓ Projected Financial Projections
- ✓ Industry-Specific Information

Executive Summary
The Executive Summary typically is the placed as the first section of your business plan, but it is the last section that you will write. Prospective investors and lenders use the Executive Summary to determine the concepts and reasonableness of your plan. Once an investor agrees to review the details of your business plan, you will probably ask the reader to sign a "Non-Disclosure" agreement that states that the reader will not release, reveal, or use any information contained in the business plan for any purpose that will interfere or compete with your company. (Seek legal counsel for guidance on using the agreement and for sample language to use in the Non-Disclosure agreement.)

Mission Statement
The mission statement is a statement of the purpose of the organization. Strategic decisions should be implemented only when they support the mission statement. Similarly, any operating procedures, goals, or internal transformations

should be abandoned if they conflict with the Mission Statement of the business.

> **"Never mistake motion for action."**
> *Famous quote by Ernest Hemingway (1899-1961)*

Market Analysis

The Market Analysis is the section of the business plan that many entrepreneurs hire consultants to complete. This section outlines the factors that define the market for your products and services. The Market Analysis typically includes a description of the regional area in which your company is located, along with a demographic assessment of the population size, the average income, the annual dollar sales of related or substitute products sold in your market, and the growth trends in the region.

> ### *Profit Opportunity*
> A Business Plan should be your description of: a) what your business will look like, b) how it will function (daily operations), c) the types of products and services it will offer, and d) the description of the customers it will serve. The business plan should create a descriptive picture of your business over each of the next five years.

If your product or service is unique in your market, then the Market Analysis will focus on the annual sales potential for all products in the industry to which your product is assigned. For example, if you are selling a unique water skiing board, then the Market Analysis will describe the annual sales level of boating accessories, the estimated number of boat owners in the area, and the anticipated growth trend over the next three years. From that global analysis, you can extract the annual sales that you anticipate for your product.

The reason that you assess the industry potential is that your unique product probably will not increase the total annual sales for the industry. Therefore, any sales that your company achieves will decrease the sales of other companies in the industry. Once you understand this level of competition, you are able to create more effective marketing plans.

For example, when the Apple® iPhone was introduced, sales of "clamshell" phones began to diminish. This trend of increasing sales of smartphones and decreasing sales of standard cell phones has continued since that point.

Company Description
The description of the company includes some demographic information, such as the name, type of entity (Partnership, LLC, Corporation, etc.), and the proposed area where the company will be located. In addition, the company description includes information about the corporate goals; mission statement; how the business will operate (e.g., heavy reliance on technology; high labor use; use of specialized trades, etc.); and how the company will address the customer base (retail, wholesale, after-market sales, discount trade sales, convention booths, internet sales, etc.). This section of your business plan can be used to give the reader a better understanding of the type of industry, the amount of start-up capital required to open the company, and the potential profit from operations.

Organization and Staffing
This section of your business plan is used to outline the management structure (owner/manager, franchise, absentee

manager, joint venture, etc.), the size of the staff, and the designated skills required for the company to be successful. Also, this section should describe the skills of the people who have agreed to be employed by the company. The business plan has greater credibility when you're able to show how the skills of your staff match the needs of the organization. In addition, when employees read how their sills are important for achieving the company's mission, they are able to build pride in their work and in their achievements without your direct input.

Financial Statement readers expect to see that the owner will be employed by the organization. However, potential investors also look for the accumulated skills and experience that the owner has attracted to start the business. An owner cannot train all staff and simultaneously open a new business. Therefore, if the owner does not have experienced employees on opening day, then the business will not be effective until all employees are fully trained and developed. A lack of training will adversely affect sales and profits.

Marketing Plan
The marketing plan includes separate sections for the timing, frequency, coverage area, and cost for:
- Public Relations campaigns.
- Advertising schedules.
- Special promotions (such as a Grand Opening, Back-to-School sale, or Holiday Season discount).
- Sales approach (direct sales, retail sales, inside sales, field sales, manufacturer's representatives, internet ad words, etc.).
- Follow-up and add-on sales efforts.

This section of the business plan should forecast the amount and structure of the sales commissions anticipated with each marketing plan. Commissions are a part of the Cost of

Discover Your Company's Strengths & Beat The Competition

Goods Sold, and a change in the amount or method of paying commissions could affect the budgeting process for the organization.

For example, many companies pay sales commissions based on a percentage of the gross invoice amount. However, if your goal in a specific marketing campaign is to build customer awareness, then your commission program may pay a fee to any employee who brings a prospective customer to a grand opening celebration.

Service or Products Offered
The product listing section of your business plan should explain the types of products that the company sells. It may also state the types of products that will not be carried. For example, a women's department store may choose to carry clothing and accessories for teens and children and it may specifically exclude jewelry from its catalog.

The products and services description helps to focus the type of marketing, supplier, company size, and investment that the company will need to start operations. For example, a wholesaler that can drop-ship from the manufacturer may only need a small sales office to flourish. Alternatively, a training center may require a large space in an office building with access to high-speed internet, satellite video transmission, and free customer parking.

Initial Capital Budget
The Initial Capital Budget includes two or more sets of financial statements. At a minimum, the budget should show the start-up capital that is required to begin operations. This means that the start-up budget will show the amount of money needed to purchase all equipment, licensing, facilities, furniture, insurance, etc. in order to open the doors on the first day. In addition, an operating budget should be included

to forecast the revenue and expense anticipated over each of the next twelve months.

These two views of the financial position of the company (start-up investment and operating activity) allows investors to assess whether the owner has the ability to organize and forecast all known expenses, to determine first year profitability, and to develop a secondary plan to address exceptional events.

Projected Financial Statements
The projected financial statements contained in your business plan present your anticipated future business results. This set of reports are different from your accounting statements in several ways.

- ♦ The projected financial statements are used to show the potential profit and return on investment based on the owner's assumptions for the future period.

- ♦ In contrast, the monthly accounting statements (that are generated from your accounting system) present an historical review of prior transactions.

The Cash Flow Statement in the business plan shows the amount of monetary resources that flow into and out from the business each month along with its associated source.

For example, the Cash Flow Statement shows the amount of funds anticipated from outside investors as a separate line item from product sales. Depreciation is excluded from the Cash Flow Statement because depreciation expense is a non-monetary transaction.

In comparison, the Statement of Cash Flows in the accounting statement shows the:

Discover Your Company's Strengths & Beat The Competition

1. Sources of working capital (decrease in Accounts Receivable, increase in Accounts Payable, loan proceeds, sales of equipment, etc.)
2. How the working capital was used during the prior period (paying debt, increase in Accounts Payable, buying real estate, etc.), and
3. A reconciliation between net income and the cash balance in the bank account.

There are many elements in common in both types of reports. In each statement, you will:

- Present income and expenses for a period of time, usually a monthly presentation over twelve to eighteen months.
- Use the same accounting choices for both statements. Therefore, if you plan to use accrual-based accounting, or if you implement straight-line depreciation to track asset value, then you should be consistent in both the accounting statements and the business plan projected financial statements.
- You can use your financial projections as the basis for your initial budget, but your actual results may influence you to change your budget once your business begins operations.

Industry-Specific Information
Industry –specific information often is included in most business plans to outline information that is unique to your industry. In this section, you may describe any regulatory restrictions that require you to use a specific process, equipment, disposal procedure, etc.

You can use this section to describe potential restrictions that affect your business, along with your plans to minimize the effects of these risks. For example, if you plan to build on a site that formerly was used as an auto repair center, many states require that you obtain a clean-soil certificate or that you perform a soil remediation to remove any hazardous chemicals before construction begins.

> *Employee Inspiration*
> The business plan has greater credibility when you are able to show how the skills of your staff match the needs of the organization. In addition, when employees read how their sills are important for achieving the company's mission, they are able to build pride in their work and in their achievements without your direct input.

The main purpose of this section is to address risks, concerns, short-term opportunities, or specific requirements of the business that investors need to know in order to make an informed decision about the risk and potential returns on their investment. When you fail to include information that a knowledgeable investor expects, then the investor may believe that you are concealing pertinent information for a disreputable reason or that you lack the necessary skills to manage the business successfully.

STRATEGIC PLAN
The strategic plan is your vision of the corporate accomplishments and how you intend to achieve these objectives. While the plan mainly contains text to describe your approach for a successful company, the strategic plan may contain a wide variety of materials. For example, your strategic plan may include market statistics, charts and diagrams to present a summary of complex data, pictures of

competitors' products, or reference lists of online information that supports the concepts in the plan (such as commercials listed on You Tube, product catalogs of competitors or suppliers, or industry trade journal articles).

Your strategic plan presents a balance between detailed steps and generic ideas. Therefore, your strategic plan should present a high-level description of: 1) your approach to succeeding (without revealing competitive secrets), 2) your unique advantages in the market, 3) your value to your customers, and 4) the primary market to which you sell.

For example, your strategic plan may include a reference that your staff will work typical business hours. This statement allows you to exclude specific start and end times and without specifically stating that the company is closed on weekends.

Conversely, your business plan should not use generic statements such as "We offer our services to all consumers with internet access" because this generic statement lacks focus and does not indicate how you will address the needs of a specific target market.

When you find the appropriate balance between the ideas and the details for your strategic plan, then you will provide others (e.g., readers, investors, employees, suppliers, bankers, etc.) with your direction for achievement and you will open opportunities for others to bring you opportunities about which you may be unaware.

BUDGETING PROCESS

When consultants suggest that a company develop a budget, staff often show resentment, resistance, or concern. This is understandable because employees typically do not have the information, authority or experience to prepare a reliable budget. When the outsider (i.e., consultant, banker, investor, or trading partner) asks the owner about the budget, there can be a similar response from the owner for the same reasons. To overcome this challenge, this section discusses the concepts of a budget and how to prepare one for your business.

There are three types of budgets that you are most likely to use in your business:

1. Operating Budget

2. Capital Budget

3. Project Budget

Each type of budget is used for a specific purpose, so they are mutually exclusive. Since you cannot substitute one type of budget for another, your company should have a current operating budget and a capital budget at all times. The project budget should be used to track a specific program (advertising campaign, new product rollout, upgrading equipment on a large scale, etc.). The Project Budget should be implemented only as needed.

Operating Budget
The operating budget is a tool used to forecast and then track the monetary impact of daily processes within your business. Specifically, the operating budget is prepared as a forecast of income and expenses for the next 18 months. Each month, the current period budget is compared to actual results and an additional forecasted period is added to the newly revised operating budget. (Some owners limit their budgets to 12 months because of the high volatility of raw materials or

market-driven prices within the industry (e.g., crude oil drillers, copper pipe manufacturers, or commercial airlines carriers.)

> *Employee Inspiration*
> When you find the appropriate balance between the ideas and the details for your strategic plan, then you can provide others (e.g., readers, investors, employees, suppliers, bankers, etc.) with your direction for achievement. Sharing this information can open opportunities for others to bring you opportunities about which you may be unaware.

For example, assume that the current period is June, 2018. On June 30, 2018, you would close the monthly accounting cycle and post the results of actual transactions. Next, you would compare the actual income and expenses accounts to the amounts that were budgeted for these items. You would compare budgeted sales to actual sales, budgeted cost of goods (COGS) sold to actual costs, and budgeted overhead expense to actual overhead disbursements. The result of the comparison is called a variance analysis.

The purpose of preparing the variance analysis is to determine whether your forecasted budget approximates the actual results of your company's operations on an ongoing basis. If the budget is not close to actual results, then you should adjust future budgets until you are able to predict, within a reasonable range, the future achievements for your business.

Positive Variance vs. Negative Variance

Discover Your Corporate Strengths & Beat The Competition

When budgeted sales are less than actual sales, the difference is referred to as a positive variance. Conversely, when budgeted revenue is lower than actual sales, then the variance is negative. For example, if your budget shows forecasted sales of $532000 for the month and your actual sales is $450,000, then the higher actual sales results in a negative variance.

For the expense accounts, when budgeted costs are higher than actual costs, the variance is positive. Conversely, when budgeted expenses are lower than actual costs, then there is a negative variance. For example, if total budgeted overhead is $375,000 and actual overhead for the period is $387,000, there is a negative variance of $12,000.

Keep in mind that a large positive variance can be as problematic as a significant negative variance. The budget is a fundamental tool to use in purchasing inventory, obtaining external financing, estimating tax payments, scheduling bonus payments to staff, planning major advertising projects, and adding capacity to meet customer demand.

Negative Budget Variance
Your planning activities (purchasing inventory, obtaining a loan, scheduling advertising, etc.) will be less effective when you incur a negative budget variance. Negative expense variance indicates that you have incurred higher costs, while negative sales variances suggest that you have missed opportunities to achieve higher sales. Either of these activities probably will result in lower profits.

Positive Budget Variance
When your budget shows a consistent positive variance in sales, then you are probably underestimating market demand in your budget. This error creates an opportunity for competitors to enter the market and take your customers

Discover Your Company's Strengths & Beat The Competition

because you may not have a sufficient sales force to meet customer demand. When customers have difficulty buying from you, then they will buy substitute products or buy from alternate vendors. In either case, a lost sale can never be recaptured. The best you can accomplish is to meet customer demand in the future.

If your expense budget shows a consistent positive balance, then you probably are minimizing discretionary costs, such as decreasing advertising, postponing store fixture updates, ignoring building maintenance, and reducing inventory levels. This approach can serve to reduce expenses in the short run, but a sustained decrease in required business costs typically results in higher future costs or reduced long-term sales.

For example, if your building maintenance is ignored for an extended period of time, then your building may require a major repair or renovation in the future to correct a major failure. This renovation may close the facility and thereby eliminate sales while the repairs are implemented. Another risk that business owners take to reduce costs is to reduce advertising spending or reduce inventory levels. This could cause your customers to transition to other vendors who continue to offer discounts, advertise on television commercials or offer a wide range of products readily available on the store shelves.

Once the variance analysis is complete, the budget is extended one month by adding a budget for the trailing month. In the above example, June has ended and July is the current month. The eighteenth month from July 2018 would be December 2019, so the owner would create a budget for December 2019 and enter that information into the 18 month budget. As each month ends, you will add one new budget period so that you are always working with an eighteen month "rolling" forecast.

As you work with the budget each month, you should see patterns that allow you to forecast more precisely. This ability to forecast will develop over time and is a necessary skill for the successful owner to master. As your accuracy improves in developing the budget, you will find it easier to discuss the value of your business to others, you will identify new opportunities for growth, and you will become better able to control your profits each year.

Bankers rely on management's ability to prepare a reliable forecast when the banker recommends a loan application for approval. If you apply for a loan with an automatic renewal or one that will be repaid over a long period of time, the bank will require periodic financial reports from your company. The bank will also require that you submit a budget for the next twelve to eighteen months.

If you show large variances with each budget presentation, bankers may feel that you are unable to manage your business in a reasonable manner. As a result, the banker may feel that your company's risk of repayment of the loan is higher than the bank's acceptable level. In this case, the bank probably would not renew a maturing loan.

Once this happens, you may find that your company will experience a cash flow crisis and that your options to obtain a bank loan or other external financing are limited or are expensive ("high risk" companies pay higher interest rates on loans than the rate that is charged to "stable" companies).

The operating budget is necessary for a company to manage its growth and stability. If you do not have an operating budget, you will be less able to notice cost increase trends, sales decrease trends, and shifts in customer demand within product categories.

Owners often dismiss the need for an operating budget when they are directly involved in the business on a daily basis. However, most automated accounting systems provide a budgeting tool that is a part of the basic software program.

One of the easiest ways to prepare an operating budget is to copy the actual results from the same month of the prior year. For example, in February 2018, you would copy the actual results from February 2017 to use as the basis for your February 2018 budget. Then, you would modify each line that requires either an increase or a decrease to match your forecast.

When that budget becomes the current plan, then you can compare your forecast to the actual results. At that point, you can adjust your expectations in the future or change operating procedures (or resources) as necessary to meet your profit goals.

Budgets can be used to manage your profits by using the budget to drive sales and expenses. However, this topic is beyond the scope of this workbook.

CAPITAL BUDGET
A Capital Budget is the tool that allows you to forecast the viability of a new investment project for your company. The capital budget typically is used to forecast the costs of transforming a major area or function of your business.

The capital budget can be used to track revenue and/or costs. For example, you can use the capital budget to estimate the cost to construct a new manufacturing plant, open a second operating office, or upgrade your technology to support internet sales worldwide.

The capital budget often is used as a substitute for a feasibility study. A feasibility study is prepared to determine whether an anticipated project will meet measureable goals. For example, companies often perform a feasibility study to forecast the number of customers anticipated to shop in one section of town, the anticipated decrease in maintenance costs that are expected by upgrading equipment, or the number of hours of labor that could be saved by automating a fabrication process

In contrast, a capital budget is used to track the costs and/or revenue that is associated with the completion of a project or program. For example, management can create a capital budget to track the cost of replacing natural gas heating units to higher efficiency electrical heating units.

During the conversion, management would use the capital budget to ensure that the project costs do not vary from the anticipated costs. Once the project is complete, management would track the future cost of utilities to determine whether the cost of the upgrade was less than the resulting decrease in utilities expense over a designated time period (e.g., two years). If this difference is positive, then the project was successful (i.e., it was economically feasible).

When a project involves creating a sales opportunity, such as opening a second office, then the capital budget could be used to track the costs of opening the office so that this cost could be depreciated over its useful life and offset against the annual operating profit of the remote office. The benefit of tracking the accumulated cost of opening a remote office is that the owner can determine the rate of return on its investment (ROI) for each location. Management would then compare the office's-specific operating profit to the cost of the office investment and the resulting percentage is the return on investment.

For example, assume that the company has invested $500,000 to build an office in City B, and this cost will be depreciated over 10 years, after which a major renovation will be required. Assumed that in Year One the office achieved sales of $750,000 for the calendar year. From this sales revenue, assume that management subtracts $500,000 for the cost of goods sold. The resulting amount of $250,000 is the Gross Profit from this location. From this amount, assume that management subtracts $160,000 for operating costs, which results in $90,000 of profit for this location. The profit could then be compared to the annual depreciation of $50,000 ($500,000 construction cost that is depreciated over 10 years yields a depreciation expense of $50,000) to yield a return on investment of 80% ($90,000 minus $50,000 is $40,000. The $40,000 return divided by $50,000 depreciation expense yields an 80% ROI).

PROJECT BUDGET
The project budget typically is used to track the cost of a specific program to ensure that the actual expense of the project does not exceed the anticipated cost. However, the project budget can be used to track revenue as well, when the project is intended to generate sales for a defined period of time. Here are two examples of a project budget.

Equipment Upgrade Project–Cost Tracking
The first example could be the upgrading of desktop computers within your company. While this project budget may focus on cost containment areas, the project may result in increased revenues or decreased operating costs that can

be tracked through the *operating budget*. Here are three ways to upgrade technology in a company.

Some companies follow the approach of upgrading one third of their desktop computers each year so that at the end of a three-year cycle everyone has an upgraded desktop computer. This approach allows the company to fund the upgrades from prior-year profits without having to obtain external financing and provides employees with current technology that is reliable.

Alternatively, some companies upgrade as a reactive solution when the technology malfunctions or the software no longer supports the daily operations. Such a reactive approach does not require a project budget because repairs and expenditures are not anticipated.

Finally, some companies upgrade their desktop computers every four to five years and implement a project to integrate the new technology into the company processes as a focused effort. Typically, this approach is used when the company transitions to a new structure (new software system, integration of multiple functions into a single software application, or automating prior manual activities).

This effort will cause a disruption of current operations and will be accompanied by staff training and data reconciliation. Without a project budget to help manage the process, the company could lose focus and spend beyond the original project estimates.

Discover Your Company's Strengths & Beat The Competition

	XYZ Sample Company						
	Project Budget-Equip Upgrade						
	February	March	April	May	June	July	Totals
Server	$2,500						$2,500
Desktops		$8,000					$8,000
Monitors		$2,500					$2,500
Wiring	$750						$750
Routers		$200					$200
Software	$6,000		$4,000	$2,500		$1,200	$13,700
Training			$3,000			$500	$3,500
Overtime			$2,500	$2,500	$2,500		$7,500
Total	$9,250	$10,700	$9,500	$5,000	$2,500	$1,700	$38,650

Each approach has benefits and challenges, so you should follow the approach that is most beneficial to your environment. For those companies that implement a wholesale upgrade every four to five years, a project budget can help ensure that the costs are contained for the upgrade.

In this example, a company may decide to upgrade all desktop computers in the accounting department. Such a project may include replacing hardware, upgrading software (newest version of the operating system and personal productivity software), and replacing obsolete applications (replacing bookkeeping software with an "enterprise resource program" or ERP).

The first step in this example project is for the owner to establish the value proposition for the project. When an owner makes a decision that is beyond the authority of the department manager, staff will seek a measure that shows the success of the project. If the value proposition is to reduce overtime by implementing a new procedure (hiring more employees, upgrading computers, introducing flextime, etc.), then staff will track their accomplishments towards this goal.

Discover Your Corporate Strengths & Beat The Competition

If the value proposition is to reduce costs in excess of the project fee, then staff can track the monetary impact of the venture. Therefore, when the owner states that the company will pay for new computers if the project is cost-effective, then employees will tend to be motivated to implement the project successfully. This enthusiasm will come from knowing that if the project fails, employees will have a more difficult effort convincing the owner to make future improvements.

In order for the value to be positive, then the resulting improvements in efficiencies, operating cost savings, or incremental revenue that results from the completed project must be higher than the cost of the project.

Once the project is approved, management should prepare an estimate of the cost of the new equipment and software from potential vendors. This research step allows employees to gain information that is not available internally and set expectations about the relative value that the company places on their responsibilities. This step may require several revisions because each vendor may offer a solution that is not directly comparable to its competitors. For example, one company may include maintenance in their initial proposal, while another vendor may include training in their proposed price.

Once the company selects the vendor who will provide the upgrades, management can prepare a budget of the cost to upgrade the desktop computers. The budget should include the equipment, software, wiring costs, supporting equipment (routers, wireless network cards, monitors, etc.) software, staff overtime for training and conversion activities, and all other costs expected for the project. In addition, the budget should show the timing of the expenditures over each month of the program. For example, equipment costs may be financed over a series of years, while overtime may occur about three months after the start of the implementation.

Each month, management should compare: 1) the budgeted costs to the actual costs, and 2) ensure that the remaining amount of the budget will be sufficient to complete the project. If the budget requires a significant modification, then the owner can plan to either accept the higher costs, obtain the necessary financing, redirect resources from other projects, or cancel or suspend the program. Without a monthly review, the owner does not have the ability to make proactive decisions about the success of the project.

Also, once the owner approves the project, staff will remain committed to the completion of the program without regard to achieving the value proposition. Therefore, staff will tend to ignore the pending failure of a project in the hope that the final results will prove positive. This is not a statement about the limitations of employees. It is a recognition of each person's role in the project.

Owners are responsible for the risk associated with decisions, while staff are responsible to carry out the duties assigned to them, without regard to financial or corporate risk. (Everyone is responsible to enhance safety, reduce product liability, and be accountable for their respective activities.)

Product Rollout Project – Revenue and Cost Tracking
The second example could be a product rollout in a new territory. Assume that you sell a consumer product that is not currently offered in a new town. The project budget can be used to show whether the completed project met the value proposition. If it did not, then management could review the activities and decide how to address the market in the next cycle (suspend deliveries, increase advertising, re-brand the product and reintroduce the line, adjust the price, etc.).

Discover Your Corporate Strengths & Beat The Competition

In this example, the owner would establish the value proposition of the project. One measure of value is to establish a minimum profit rate that will sustain sales in the new town. Another value proposition is to establish a minimum level of incremental sales of all products in the town that result from the introduction of the new product. (Incremental sales can increase when the new product complements existing products and both products can be sold as a bundled item or sold at a discounted price). Other value propositions may be based on creating a market over time, such as when a town first installs cable television access services. The early years may be unprofitable, but the company may expect to earn profits after three years and then be profitable every year afterwards.

Once the value proposition is established, the project budget is created to forecast the costs of the program and revenue to be earned over a specified timeframe. Each month, management should compare: 1) the budgeted costs to the actual costs, and 2) ensure that the remaining amount of the budget will be sufficient to support the completed project.

If the budget requires a significant modification, then the owner can accept the higher costs; obtain the necessary financing, redirect resources from other projects; or cancel or suspend the program. Without a monthly review, the owner does not have the ability to make proactive decisions about the success of the project.

When management monitors the budgets monthly, then staff can reduce cost overruns by implementing corrective action. If sales results fail to achieve projected levels, employees can increase sales activities by offering introductory discounts, employing more direct sales staff, increasing the frequency of advertising that focuses on benefits, or modifying the product delivery to match customer needs (offering weekend installations, scheduling installation dates sooner, etc.).

CONCLUSION
This section started with a description of the SWOT Analysis that business owners can use to assess their strengths, weaknesses, opportunities, and threats. Through this analysis, owners can create a plan to maximize their success by exploiting the company's areas of expertise, reducing its vulnerabilities, exploring new areas of profitability, and making long-term modifications to address potential concerns.

The main benefit of the SWOT Analysis is to support the owner's proactive steps in managing the long-term success of the company. Successful owners recognize that market factors can reduce or eliminate profits in any single year. However, successful owners will address this issue by maintaining an adequate line of credit or cash reserves to cover expenses during these temporary down turns.

Chapter 2
Finding The Money

After you decide to start a business, you will need a source of funding, called start-up capital. You will use the cash to buy furniture, equipment, raw materials or inventory, software, signs, etc. In many cases, the owner will invest personal assets and then seek additional external financing in order to accumulate the total amount of funds needed to start the business. The traditional sources of money include:

- Personal Savings
- Family Loan
- Bank Loan
- Credit Cards
- Investor Capital

Each of these financing sources holds unique implications that the owner should consider before requesting and accepting the money. In addition to start-up capital, most businesses will need external financing to support significant growth once it has achieved sustainability. (Sustainability is the level at which current operating profits are sufficient to support operating activity in the next cycle that will generate a consistent profit margin.)

PERSONAL SAVINGS
The easiest source of capital to find is your own savings. Once you are committed to starting a business, it's easy to justify investing your own wealth into the business with the expectation that you'll receive high rewards from successful operations.

Discover Your Company's Strengths & Beat The Competition

If you plan to seek external financing, then you should understand that bankers and investors typically shy away from providing capital to business owners who do not invest their own capital into the business. The common thinking from bankers is that if you lack the ability to accumulate wealth in the form of personal savings or if you lack the conviction to risk your own money in the business, then why should someone else take a chance on your ability to succeed in the business venture?

> *Profit Opportunity*
> If you plan to seek external financing, then you should understand that bankers and investors typically shy away from providing capital to business owners who do not invest their own capital into the business. The common thinking from bankers is that if you lack the ability to accumulate wealth in the form of personal savings or if you lack the conviction to risk your own money in the business, then why should someone else take a chance on your ability to succeed in the venture?

The second major issue to consider is that when you invest your savings in the business, you automatically limit your ability to address future cash flow shortages, slow business trends, or unexpected expenses. Therefore, you should consider your options carefully before investing any amount of your personal savings into a business.

FAMILY LOAN

Entrepreneurs often have the ability to convince others that their idea for a business holds minimal risk. Their enthusiasm is infectious, their view of the world is positive, and their understanding of people is extensive. Therefore, when a new business owner approaches a family member for a loan, the investing relative often will see this opportunity as a guarantee of wealth.

There is an old adage that "you should never do business with family or friends." The main reason for this rule is that the corporate financing arrangement with family or friends often is informal, the work effort is not clearly explained, and the business risks and outcomes are not specifically defined. For this reason, you should refrain from asking for help from "related investors" unless you offer the same arrangement that an unrelated investor would find attractive.

When you ask a family member to invest in your business, you already have a relationship with that person. The relative or friend knows you; he or she is comfortable with your personality; you and your benefactor have common life experiences; and you have built a level of mutual trust based on prior interactions. As a result of this familiarity, you may feel that you can ask a friend or a family member a question or hold a conversation without including many of the details that would be required when first meeting a potential business associate.

In reality, when there is only an informal agreement, the expectations of the borrower often are different from the expectations of the lender. When there is unclear or missing information, each party tends to make assumptions about how the agreement will be implemented, and these assumptions will be biased toward the person making the assumptions. Once these parties begin to act on their own assumptions, each party tends to feel cheated as the business progresses, regardless of the outcome of the transaction.

For example, assume that you borrow $25,000 from a favorite cousin to start your business. Three potential outcomes are: 1) you will earn a profit and repay the loan, 2) you will earn a profit but you will lack sufficient cash to repay the loan timely, or 3) your business will lose money and you will be unable to repay the loan.

Under scenario number one, if you did not discuss the interest rate clearly then your repayment of the loan probably will not meet your cousin's expectations for the financial transaction. Your cousin may believe that he is due a higher interest rate (especially if he/she believes that you are earning a high salary and both parties did not agree to a specific interest rate).

If your cousin assumed the money was an exchange for an ownership position, then he/she may feel that the repayment is an unacceptable repurchase of the cousin's assumed high-value ownership position.

If either of the other two scenarios occur and you cannot repay the loan, you may take the position that your business made an unsecured loan from your cousin, and therefore, the company has no legal requirement to pay. Under this assumption, you may feel that your cousin should not expect repayment because the business is not able to repay the loan and that you should not be held personally responsible for a business loan.

When you fail to repay your cousin, then he or she probably will be angry with you for not repaying his loan principle and anticipated interest. This anger may be displayed at family events and probably will diminish your positive interactions with your cousin for many months.

Discover Your Corporate Strengths &
Beat The Competition

Another issue that often results when family members become investors in your company is that family investors may not understand the reality of a business investment. Family investors often assume that their investment in your company is as safe as investing in a certificate of deposit at a bank and that monthly dividends will be issued before any business expenses are covered. In addition, family investors, who are partial owners of the business, often feel that they have a right to make decisions about daily operations, capital improvement, and staffing issues.

Finally, family investors may attempt to coerce the owner by implying that other family members will disapprove of the owner's actions without the investor's support. This tacit form of intimidation can place undue stress on the owner or may alter the timing or method used to address a current business problem.

In contrast to the family investor, when you seek financial support from a knowledgeable outside investor, that person will require a formal agreement in advance of any monetary exchange. The agreement should specify the actions, level of authority, ownership rights, and expectations of each party (including anticipated rewards or future cash payments). A well-written agreement will not solve all problems, but it will reduce the ambiguity when you give the investor a status report about your business.

Family loans often are supported by unclear communication, which is an improper approach to running a business. Therefore, you should refrain from conducting business with friends and family unless you can conduct the transaction under the same conditions as you would conduct business with non-related suppliers or customers.

BANK LOANS

Bank loans are commonly used to: a) finance a business as a start-up strategy, b) to provide working capital to support an operating plan, c) to support the investment in long-term equipment that is used to generate future income, and d) purchase real estate, such as an office building or a production plant. The two most common types of bank loans are the term loan and line of credit. The first type, a term loan, typically is issued by the bank to fund the company's purchase of a large asset (real estate, large equipment, expanded warehouse construction, etc.). A term loan is designed be repaid in equal monthly payments over a period of 5, 10, 15, or 20 years.

> *Profit Opportunity*
> There is an old adage that "you should never do business with family or friends." The main reason for this rule is that the corporate financing arrangement with family or friends often is informal, the work effort is not clearly explained, and the business risks and outcomes are not specifically defined. For this reason, you should refrain from enlist help from "related investors" unless you offer the same arrangement that an unrelated investor would find attractive.

Under the concept of a term loan, a borrower will request an amount of money with a plan to buy a large asset that will be used to reduce operating cost or help to generate income. For example, a company may want to buy a building (instead of renting an office) in order to reduce its monthly operating costs while building equity (ownership value) in the property. Alternatively, the owner may want to borrow money to purchase new machinery that will be used to fabricate inventory items that will be sold at a profitable rate. In either case, the cost savings or the profits generated from the asset purchase will be used to repay the loan, which consists of interest and principle payments.

Originally, term loans that were issued for 10 – 20 years carried terms that did not change. That is, the borrower paid a monthly loan payment amount that was predetermined and continued the payments over the life of the loan (without the expectation of paying the loan before its maturity date).

In the late 1970s and early 1980s, interest rates began to increase radically each month. During this period, bankers began to feel that issuing a long-term loan with a fixed interest rate was highly risky. (Banks earn a profit by lending money to borrowers at a rate that is higher than the percentage that is paid to savings customers.) In a period when interest rates are rising, banks had to pay higher interest to savings account holders, but they could not afford this payment based on the income from loan payments that were issued with lower rates from the prior year.

To reduce their risk, banks began issuing term loans with variable interest rate and balloon payments prior to maturity. For example, under a variable rate loan, a borrower will request a $25,000 loan. The bank will issue the loan with terms such as "New York Prime rate plus 2.5 points." This phrase would mean that the bank would establish the interest rate as the amount that the best borrowers can negotiate with the international bank offices in New York plus 2 ½ percentage points above that prime rate. If the New York Prime is 6%, then the loan term would be 8.5% at the date of closing.

This rate (8.5% in our example) would remain in effect until the loan rate expires or renews (at the end of every three month period) or until the loan fully matures or is fully paid. At renewal, if the New York Prime climbs to 7.75%, then the loan interest rate will be reset to 10.25% for the next three month cycle and the payments will be recalculated on the remaining loan balance at this renewed rate.

Some customers like the variable rate loans because when interest rates drop, then the loan payments are reduced as well. Also, customers were enticed to accept a variable rate loan because the initial interest rate was lower than the quoted rate for a traditional Fixed Rate term loan.

This approach worked well for a few years, until the market fell into a severe recession in the mid 1980's. At that time, customers (who had high credit ratings when they first applied for the loan) sustained losses during the recession and could not repay their loans. As a result of the loan defaults, many banks and savings and loan institutions sustained lower profits and some suffered losses that resulted in the bank's failure.

Since that time, many changes have been implemented. Banks continue to offer both variable rate and fixed rate business loans, but many of these loans include a balloon payment at the end of five years. A balloon payment for a loan means that the loan payment will be calculated based on the full term of the loan. However, at the end of the balloon term (five years in this example), the loan balance will become fully payable.

Discover Your Corporate Strengths & Beat The Competition

When the balloon payment is due, the borrower has three options. The Borrower can:

1. Pay the loan balance in full;

2. Obtain a new loan at the terms in effect at that time to continue the financing arrangement, or

3. Default on the loan and risk losing the collateral used to support the loan.

In 2012 banks commonly issue a term loan with a 15 year amortization and a 5 year balloon note. In this example, the bank would loan an amount to a borrower and calculate the repayment terms based on a 15 year repayment schedule. The borrower would make monthly payments based on this calculated amount for five years (or 60 months). At the end of the 5 year period, the bank would contact the borrower to renegotiate the loan. The bank would offer a replacement 15-year loan based on the company's current credit score, the current interest rates and a 5-year balloon payment.

This approach of issuing a long-term loan that will expire in a few years allows the bank to adjust its interest rate (and profitability) to reflect the capital market conditions.

* * * * *

The second type of bank loan is a line of credit. Under the terms of a line of credit, a company is issued a maximum loan credit amount. At any time, the company can withdraw an amount of money against a line of credit until it reaches its total available limit. Each month, the company is assessed an interest charge based on the total amount of money that has been withdrawn from the available limit but has not been repaid. (Interest is calculated based on the loan's open balance each month.)

Finding The Money

For example, assume that your company is issued a $50,000 line of credit, and you have transferred $5,000 from this line of credit into your cash account. At the end of month one, the bank will charge your company an interest fee based on a $5,000 outstanding balance that was borrowed from the total line of credit.

Next, assume that you withdraw an additional $15,000 from the line of credit in the second month. At the end of the second month, the company will be assessed an interest fee based on a $20,000 outstanding balance that has been withdrawn from a line of credit ($5,000 withdrawn in the first month plus $15,000 withdrawn in the second month equals the total outstanding balance of $20,000 at the end of month two).

Next, assume that the company repays the $20,000 that it has borrowed on the first day of the third month. At the end of the third month, the company will not be assessed an interest fee because the outstanding balance on the line of credit was zero throughout the third month. Under this scenario, the company would have no further interest fees assessed until it withdraws another sum of money from the line of credit.

CREDIT CARDS
Entrepreneurs often consider credit cards an acceptable form of external financing for their business. Credit cards are readily available as unsecured lines of credit to anyone with an adequate credit rating.

When a credit card is used to purchase items for a business, the credit card will have an established maximum credit limit available to the cardholder in the same way that a line of credit will start with a maximum credit limit. Each time the cardholder makes a purchase using a credit card, the available limit is reduced by the amount of the outstanding debt associated with a credit card. In addition, the cardholder is assessed an interest fee for each month in which there is an outstanding balance due to the credit card company.

While credit cards are an easy form of external financing, they tend to be a poor choice of financing for a business. Credit cards fees and interest rates typically are significantly higher than the rates that are available through banks for a traditional line of credit. Therefore, companies should refrain from using credit cards to finance their company's debt when bank loans are available at a lower cost.

The author recognizes that credit card purchases are often used as a substitute for a purchase order system (because all purchases are documented) and are used as a temporary form of cash. If the business owner is able to repay the total balance due on the credit cards each month without incurring an interest fee, then credit cards may be a convenient alternative to purchasing items using cash or a company check.

Keep in mind that the undisciplined entrepreneur can quickly become dependent on the use of credit cards because of the convenience and high maximum available balance. More than one business has failed because the owner lost track of spending trends that resulted in high credit card debt that could not be repaid through existing profits.

INVESTOR CAPITAL
The last type of external financing is investor capital. As the owner of the business, you can elect to sell a portion of your business to others on a short-term basis or on a permanent basis.

Venture Capitalists often seek to invest in a new or growing company for a limited period of time. Typically, the investor will seek a relatively high dividend for five to seven years and then expect the company to repurchase the investor's stock at the prevailing market value. This allows the entrepreneur to obtain investor capital to start a business or to expand operations without bank financing and then share the profits with the investor. After a predetermined number of years, the company can buy back the investor's stock and the entrepreneur will become the majority owner once again.

When a business is profitable, or holds a high potential for profits, investors will be attracted to finance the business. One of the benefits of taking on additional owners is that the new owners can add different skills to the executive management team. .

* * * * *

FINANCING DECISIONS IMPACT EMPLOYEES
During the initial planning for the business it's difficult to see, but improper financing can create negative employee morale. When a company is either undercapitalized (operating with insufficient funds) or over leveraged (incurring debt that cannot be paid through current operations), the owner will be stressed and will tend to make short-term decisions that may confuse workers.

Anytime an owner implements inconsistent or incongruent policies, staff will tend to limit their emotional commitment to the organization and this will limit their ability to help the company achieve its goals. For instance, when an owner accepts family investors into the company because bank loans are not available, then the decision-making process may become unclear as family members attempt to exert power or influence without the owner's knowledge or approval. This occurs because the family members may not make objective business decisions.

For example, assume that the owner borrows $150,000 from a retired Uncle to start a business. If the Uncle is concerned about the stability of his investment, he may visit the company unannounced, question employees about their procedures, and begin making "suggestions" about how to handle specific customer requests for service.

> *Employee Inspiration*
> When the owner implements inconsistent or incongruent policies, staff will tend to limit their emotional commitment to the organization and this will limit their ability to help the company achieve its goals.

While the Uncle may believe that his actions are helpful and insightful, this effort will tend to confuse and frustrate employees who will question the lines of authority, the nature of the Uncle's ownership, and the owner's ability to control the company's operations.

This set of activities and impact probably would not occur if the owner had borrowed a sufficient amount of capital from an independent investor based on a clear business agreement. An experienced investor would not assume a level of authority greater than is stated in the lending agreement, and an independent investor would have communicated his questions, concerns, and advice directly to the owner without involving staff.

CONCLUSION

Under the capitalistic concept of business, an entrepreneur or syndicate will start a business using a combination of the owner's personal wealth and investor financing. The start-up funds will be used to purchase or produce goods and services that will be offered to the market at a price that is higher than the company's costs. The profits from this endeavor will then be used to finance operations in the next cycle to create a sustainable company.

When a company is ready to grow beyond its current operating level, it will require additional resources to achieve this growth. The increased resources (additional staff, higher inventory levels, more storage, etc.) typically are purchased with prior year accumulated profits or with additional external financing. Growth, in this context, is the ability to grow beyond an incremental increase in profits. Such a significant increase in company profits requires a structural change in the company, and this level of improvement is not financed through current operating profit.

When a company is ready to accept external financing it has five main sources of financing:

- Personal Savings
- Family Loan
- Bank Loan
- Credit Cards
- Investor Capital

Each of these sources are valid forms of external financing, and each one holds unique challenges for the owner to convince others to invest in the company and for the company to repay the loans.

* * * * *

APPENDIX
ADDITIONAL SOURCES OF ASSISTANCE

Here are some free resources that you may find helpful in your continued educational endeavors.

SMALL BUSINESS DEVELOPMENT CENTER (SBDC)
Since 1983, the SBDC has provided small business assistance to potential entrepreneurs and existing small businesses. The 63 Lead centers are located in many metropolitan cities to provide confidential, one-on-one business counseling at no cost to small business owners or entrepreneurs.

Each center provides low-cost business training through seminars. While the course topics are unique to each center, here are some of the topics that may be offered:

- Understanding Financial Statements
- Improving Your Ability to Obtain A Bank Loan
- Developing A Marketing Plan
- Building a Strategic Business Plan
- Implementing accounting Software

Visit the WWW.SBA.GOV website to learn about the range of services offered through the SBDC. The website at www.asbdc-us.org/ can help you find a center close to you.

U.S. SMALL BUSINESS ADMINISTRATION (SBA)
The SBA offers specific programs to small business owners to help educate and finance the company's operations. The SBA Emerging 200 Initiative is focused on executives of established businesses, currently poised for growth, from communities across the country and provides them the organizational framework, resource network, and motivation required to build a sustainable business of size and scale.

In addition, the SBA offers direct business loans to organizations that have sustained a loss from a Presidentially Declared Disaster. Finally, the SBA offers a guarantee program for companies seeking a business loan from participating lending institutions. Specifically, a company with marginal credit may qualify under the program to have the SBA guarantee a portion of the loan repayment to the lender in the event that the company is unable to pay the loan balance. (This option is offered through the SBA Loan Guarantee program. It is not an SBA loan.)

The website at WWW.SBA.GOV offers a range of assistance to small business owners, including a business plan development tool, a search engine to find potential grants and loans for small businesses, and a basic primer on developing a marketing plan.

AMERICAN INSTITUTE OF CERTIFIED PUBLIC ACCOUNTANTS (AICPA)
The AICPA offers financial literacy education through its 360 Degrees of Financial Literacy initiative. This initiative sends the message that financial education should be a lifelong endeavor——from encouraging children to save their allowance to helping adults plan for a secure retirement.

The information is directed toward consumers, but you can use the concepts in your business to help you budget your income and invest your profits.

YAHOO FINANCE
The www.Finance.Yahoo.com website offers news headlines and other financial information that businesses can use. From the information on the website, you can learn how to read annual financial statements and then access the annual reports of public companies in your industry. This is a two - step process. First, search for Annual Financial Statements using the search tool and read the article on understanding financial statements. Next, use the search tool to find the annual reports for the target company.

Every company can compare its in-house financial results to a public counterpart by transforming the dollar amounts to percentages and by calculating key financial ratios. For example, if you restate each line of your profit and loss statement as a percentage of sales (divide the line item amount by the total sales amount for the same period), then you can compare that percentage value to the similar value for a public corporation. (Most accounting software can generate percentage-based financial statements automatically.)

Comparing key ratios, such as Return on Equity (Net Income divided by Equity), Debt Ratio (Liabilities divided by Assets), or Profit Margin Analysis (Gross Profit divided by Sales), allows you to determine how your company compares to the national companies in your industry. With this information, you can determine whether you are operating as effectively as the larger, publically traded organizations.

ENTREPRENEUR.COM

This website at www.entrepreneur.com offers many articles and news videos about business topics, such as leadership, human resources, social entrepreneurship, etc.

IRS.GOV

The website WWW.IRS.GOV is the main source of tax forms and tax information for businesses. You can download .PDF versions of most federal tax forms and you can check out the status of new decisions implemented by the Internal Revenue Service.

For example, if your business was impacted by a weather event that has been designated as a Presidentially Declared Disaster, then you may qualify for extended filing deadlines for your income tax, payroll, or other filings. You can also apply for a Federal Employer Identification Number that most banks require before your business can open a checking account.

All information on the website is free and often the information you need can be found on the website as an alternative to calling the IRS. This can be a big time saver and can answer questions when the IRS is closed.

BUSINESS.USA.GOV

This website is a product of collective thoughts and inputs from multiple federal agencies. These agencies have pledged their commitment to making this site a one-stop shop for everything related to business in the USA: The site promises to use technology to create a one-stop platform to make it easier than ever for businesses to access services to help them grow and hire.

ALLBUSINESS.COM

This website offers a series of articles about business. The website is well organized, and the diversity of articles will keep you interested well into the morning hours of your web surfing activity. You can use the Search bar to find articles on a specific target, or you can use the menu buttons to find articles within a general area (such as Sales, Technology, or Staffing).

This page left blank intentionally.

Check out Richard Melancon's first book on
Personal Money Management for
Those in Financial Crisis:

YOU <u>CAN</u> AFFORD THE GOOD LIFE

Richard Melancon, CPA wrote his first book, "You <u>Can</u> Afford the Good Life" to help individuals who are in financial crisis and want to manage the money they have to achieve the goals they desire. The book describes how people have changed their view of money from an investment tool to a consumption activity, and how this change has reduced consumers' ability to manage their income. This shift has created a dependency on credit cards and excessive debt.

Success is universally desired, but it is defined uniquely by each individual. This book is a tool for you to set goals, see alternatives to current spending patterns, and build a successful life according to your definition.

When you fail to manage your money,
Others control your happiness.

Find out how to live a good life without having to earn more money.

Purchase your copy of
"You <u>Can</u> Afford the Good Life"
today from Amazon.com and www.ramcpa.com

Check out Richard Melancon's Leadership book:

Integrity-Based Leadership
Propel Your Company to the Top of Your Industry

- Want more Profit?
- Want to attract employees who want to help your company succeed?
- Want customers to be your biggest cheerleaders and help find more customers?

Start using Integrity-based Leadership today. Align your values and priorities with the corporate mission. Use Honesty, Clarity, Transparency and High Ethical Values in all of your business transactions. Leave your competition behind as they try to catch up with you (instead of undercutting your price…*and your profit*).

Buy your copy today:
www.Amazon.com
or
www.ramcpa.com

In 2010, Richard A Melancon, CPA wrote the comprehensive guide to building a great business. It is available at www.amazon.com The title of that book is:

18 Secrets to Unlock Profit and Inspire Employees

With enough time and money, anyone can have a successful business. But if you are like 99.5% of other business owners, you do not have unlimited time or money to waste. The books covers all significant areas of business so that you can build a successful and sustainable business in the least amount of time.

In order to cover all areas of business, the book is 476 pages long. However, most business owners have some of the skills covered in the book and may not need to improve their talents in every area. For this reason, Mr. Melancon published the following seven books based largely on the content of the comprehensive book from 2010.

Book 1 **Discover Your Company's Strengths & Beat the Competition**
This book will help you build a SWOT Analysis (Strengths, Weaknesses, Opportunities, and Weaknesses) and identify sources of funding for your business when you are ready to grow.

Book 2 **Sales - The Primary Driver of Success**
True business growth is achieved by increasing your sales not reducing costs. This book helps you define each of your sales activities so that you are spending your time and money effectively.

Book 3 **Focus on Profit**
Every business owner looks at the Net Profit as soon as the Income Statement is printed. But, this number is the least important number on the statement because it is a historical

number that cannot be changed. This book shows you how to manage your profit before the month begins so that you are not disappointed when the profits fall below your expectations. The book unveils the concepts that owners need to know when the financial statements are printed each month.

This is not an accounting book. It is a tool to give you the insight about the profit drivers in your business to beat the competition.

Book 4 **Is an LLC the Right Choice**
Many people choose to form their business as an LLC without knowing if this is the correct choice for them. This book offers a clear definition of the four basic entity types and how to choose the correct type for your business. If you have any plans to: a) retire by selling your business, b) add partners who will increase bottom line profit, or c) merge with another company so that you can leverage your success and build profit in another location, then this book is a must read.

Book 5 **Rules of Engagement**
One of the least understood details are the rules to opening a business. The rules often seem mysterious and unreasonable. This book explains the regulations that all businesses must follow to keep from being penalized or closed by the government. If you have ever wondered how you benefit from the business laws, this book will answer all of your basic questions, and probably many more.

Book 6 **Money Matters - Cash is King**
One of the most often asked questions from new business owners is: "Why is my cash balance different from my Net Profit?" This book answers this and many other questions related to managing the cash in your business. Having cash allows you to: a) grow profit, b) add customers, c) build multiple locations, d) add staff to reduce your stress, and e)

invest in resources to reduce costs. *Without sufficient cash, your business is doomed.* If you have any questions about your cash flow – and why it is never available when it is needed, then buy this book today.

Book 7 **Staff Are Your Greatest Resource**

If you want to grow beyond the startup stage to achieve your dreams, you will need staff.

- Employees allow you to operate your business while you are on vacation.
- Staff continue to generate sales while you are busy negotiating a lease with a new landlord.
- Workers help ensure that customers receive the products and service for which they paid.

Bottom line: Treat your staff like they matter and they will exceed your expectations. Treat them like a cost, and they will resent you. They will refuse to work above minimal levels. And, they will ignore any potential to help you reduce cost, increase profit or build an exceptional business.

This book is a must if you have ever wondered how to delegate tasks to others while ensuring quality in your business.

Coming soon, Richard A Melancon, CPA will release a set of training videos on **Starting a Successful Business.**

For more information, visit www.ramcpa.com

www.ingramcontent.com/pod-product-compliance
Lightning Source LLC
Chambersburg PA
CBHW071422220526
45469CB00004B/1397